T0132189

WHAT CAN I DO TODAY?

Rita T. Matz

Order this book online at www.trafford.com
or email orders@trafford.com

Most Trafford titles are also available at major online book retailers.

Printed in the United States of America.

ISBN: 978-1-4669-8324-3 (sc)
ISBN: 978-1-4669-8325-0 (e)

Library of Congress Control Number: 2013904173

Trafford rev. 04/19/2013

Dedication

Thank you to my Guru, Don, who has helped me so very much in so many ways, to be able to publish my book.

This book is for my children, Wendy, Beverly and Lori and for my beautiful grandchildren who have been exposed to the activities in this book over the many years.

I also want to thank my friend Ella, for all her help.

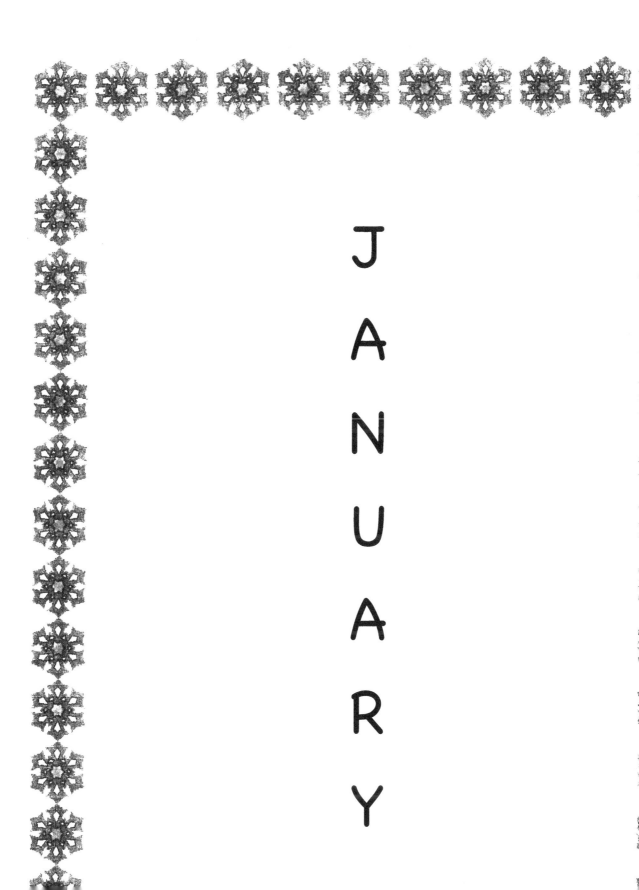

JANUARY

SNOW MAN OR SNOW LADY

Articles Needed:

(Note:) This activity may be used with or without the electrical parts.

Wide necked bottle
Clear Christmas ball to set on neck
Cord with clear Christmas bulb or small 15W bulb
Red felt or red stocking for hat
Red felt for scarf and earmuffs
Two jewels for eyes
Black buttons
Heavy wire or coat hanger for arms
Spray snow

Insert light bulb inside bottle and let hang out over top of bottle and tape down on bottle sides.

Place clear Christmas bail or any other type ball, if not using electricity, on top of bottle and tape down on neck of bottle.

Place a wire, about 12", around shoulders of bottle to front, on both sides, for arms. Tape securely to bottle.

Cover all with cotton batting, starting at top.
Cut out felt scarf for around neck.
Cut out red hat or use red stocking.
Cut out large red circles for earmuffs.
Glue two jewels for eyes.
Glue black buttons for buttons of snowman.
Use red felt or small black buttons for mouth.
Use larger black button for nose.
Spray with snow, if desire and let dry.
Plug in and light up snowman.

SNOWFLAKES

Articles needed:

    White paper
    Scissors
    String
    Tape

Cut white paper into a square.
Fold in half diagonally.
Cross left point over to right side.
Cross right point over to left side.
Cut points, dipping in center.
Cut out small shapes, such as circles, triangles or squares.
Cut out small half circle at center and bottom of folded paper.
Open to a six pointed snowflake.
Hang with string or tape on window.

cut

POETRY

Articles needed:

> Poetry book
> Blue, black or brown construction paper
> Poem "Fenceposts" run off on computer
> Crayons or magic markers
> Spray snow
> Glue

Read "Fenceposts" several times.
Discuss poem.
Run poem off on computer.
Illustrate poem on dark construction paper.
Spray with snow spray and let dry.
Glue poem to bottom of illustrated construction paper.

FEBRUARY

CALENDAR

Articles Needed:

      February Calendar
      Blue construction paper
      Pink Construction paper
      Red construction paper
      White construction paper
      Green construction paper

Run off February calendar.
Glue calendar to blue construction paper.
Cut out various sizes of heart flowers in pink white and red.
Glue heart flowers on blue construction paper.
Use green construction paper for sterns and leaves.
Make leaves in green heart shapes.
Glue sterns and leaves onto flowers.
Make green irregular grass at bottom edge and as wide as the blue construction paper.
Glue to blue paper at bottom.

SEEDS

Articles Needed:

    Seeds
    Egg carton
    Top soil
    Water
    Paper
    Pencil

Discuss seeds and their needs.
Using egg cartons, fill with top soil.
Place seeds in each section of carton.
Water slightly.
Place on sill or appropriate place for sun and light.
On paper, record date of planting and dates thereafter of growth.

STORY ABOUT GROUNDHOG

"WILL SPRING BE EARLY OR WILL IT BE LATE?"

Articles Needed:

Story—"Will Spring Be Early Or Will It Be Late?"
Blue construction paper
White construction paper
Small piece of brown construction paper
Very small piece of green construction paper
Very small piece of red construction paper or red crepe paper
Scissors
Glue

Read story and discuss it.

Use blue construction paper for background.

Using white construction paper, cut out a piece as wide as the blue paper and about 3" high, cutting it unevenly for a blanket of snow.

Using brown construction paper, cut out a very small, upright groundhog.

Make a small slit in the snow and pass the groundhog through slit from back to front.

Make a very small red flower with green stem.

Glue flower on snow facing groundhog.

Cut out or draw brown, bare trees.

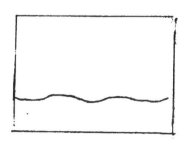

LINCOLN'S BIRTHDAY

Articles Needed:

> Story about Lincoln
> Pattern of Lincoln's head
> Black construction paper
> Lined paper
> Scissors
> Pencil
> Glue

Read story of Lincoln and discuss.
Using black construction paper and pencil, trace around Lincoln's head.
Cut out.
Using lined paper, write four sentences about
Lincoln.
Glue lined paper to bottom of portrait.

ABRAHAM LINCOLN

Our 16th president
1809-1865

Trace and cut out the silhouette of Abraham Lincoln on black construction paper. Mount the silhouette on white construction paper.

WASHINGTON'S BIRTHDAY

Articles Needed:

    Story about Washington
    Pattern of Washington's head
    White construction paper
    Lined paper
    Scissors
    Pencil
    Glue
    Crayons

Read story of Washington and discuss.
Using white construction paper and pencil, trace around Washington's head.
Cut out.
Using lined paper, write four sentences about
Washington.
Glue lined paper to portrait.
Decorate around edges of lined paper with hatchets and cherries with sterns.

THE FATHER OF OUR COUNTRY

George Washington

Articles Needed:

    Black construction paper
    Red or blue construction paper

Trace and cut out this silhouette of George Washington on black construction paper. Mount the silhouette on blue or red construction paper.

FLAG FOR PRESIDENT'S DAY

Articles Needed:

> White construction paper
> Red construction paper
> Blue constructions paper
> White chalk or white crayon
> Scissors
> Glue

Use white construction paper for background and hold horizontally.

Cut out seven narrow red strips, the width of the horizontal white paper.

Glue one red strip along edge at top and bottom of white paper.

Leave same width of white paper showing, for white stripes.

Glue two more red strips, one at top and one at bottom.

Leave same width of white paper and glue two more red strips, one at top and one at bottom.

Glue last red strip in remaining area, leaving the same amount of white showing above and below last strip.

Cut out rectangle of blue paper, almost half the width of the flag and large enough to include fourth stripe down from top, right along edge.

Glue rectangle to left side of flag.

Use white chalk or white crayon to make 50 stars or dots to represent stars.

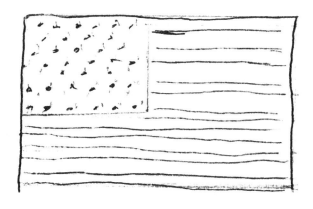

ABRAHAM LINCOLN

Our 16th president
1809-1865

Trace and cut out the silhouette of Abraham Lincoln on black construction paper. Mount the silhouette on white construction paper.

LOG CABIN FOR LINCOLN'S BIRTHDAY

Articles Needed:

    Black construction paper
    Brown construction paper
    Orange construction paper
    Scissors
    Pencil
    Crayons
    Glue

Use black construction paper for background.

Construct log cabin using brown uneven strips of paper, making roof and side of cabin.

Glue on black background as constructing.

Draw a side view of a stoned chimney, using brown construction paper.

Draw large stones with black crayon.

Cut out chimney.

Glue chimney to side of log cabin.

Cut out two windows on side of cabin.

Turn project over and glue orange paper behind cut out windows to look like a fire burning within cabin.

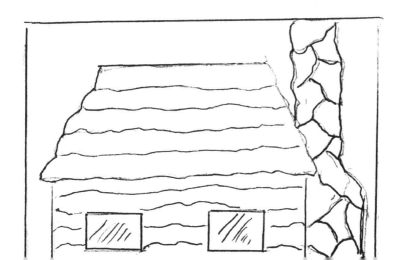

VALENTINES

Articles Needed:

   Red construction paper
   String or ribbon
   Scissors
   Glue

Using large red construction paper, cut out a large heart.
Continue cutting out hearts until they get very small.
Glue each cut out heart, from large to small on ribbon or string and hang.

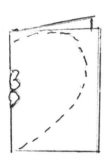

VALENTINE BUTTERFLIES

Articles Needed:

Red construction paper
Pink construction paper
Scissors
Glue
Yarn or string

Cut out two large red hearts the same size.
Cut out one heart from each of these.
Using the outer edges of each heart, glue together at points, forming wings.
Cut out two more red hearts from remaining hearts.
Using outer edges of these hearts, glue together at points and glue on top of other points of larger heart, forming double wings.
Using pink construction paper cut out small heart.
Glue small heart over points of hearts to form body.
Cut out two small straight pieces of paper for antennae.
Glue antennae to top of body.
Cut out two very tiny, pink hearts.
Glue each tiny, pink heart to the end of each antennae.
Hang with yarn or string.

VALENTINE TURTLE

Articles Needed:

Red construction paper
Pink construction paper
Scissors
Glue

Cut large red heart for body.
Cut small red heart for head.
Glue head to body, opposite point of heart.
Cut two very small pink hearts for eyes.
Glue eyes to either side of head.
Cut very small pink heart and glue to point of body for a tail.
Cut four small pink hearts for feet.
Glue feet to body.

VALENTINE CAT

Articles Needed:

    Red construction paper
    Pink construction paper
    Scissors
    Glue

Cut red heart for head.
Cut two small pink hearts for ears.
Cut very small pink hearts for eyes, nose and mouth.
Glue ears to top of head.
Glue eyes to head.
Invert nose and glue to head.
Glue mouth to head.
Cut very thin strips of pink paper for whiskers.
Glue whiskers under nose.
Cut long red heart for body.
Fold in half and invert.
Glue head to point of folded, red heart.
Cut one long, thin red heart for tail.
Glue tail to round side of folded heart at bottom.
Cut one long, very thin, red heart for feet.
Lay sidewards, opposite tail, at bottom of body and glue.

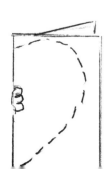

VALENTINE HEART MAN OR LADY

Articles Needed:

        Red construction paper
        White construction paper
        Scissors
        Glue
        Yarn or string

Cut large red heart for head.
Cut smaller white heart for hat on head.
Glue hat to head.
Cut small white hearts for eyes, nose and mouth.
Cut out rectangle from white paper for body.
Glue head to top of rectangle.
Cut out two 8" x 1" white strips for arms.
Accordion pleat arms and glue to each side of body at shoulders.
Cut out two small red hearts for hands.
Glue hands to bottom of arms.
Cut out two 10" x 1" white strips for legs.
Accordion pleat legs and glue to bottom of rectangle.
Cut out two small red hearts for feet.
Glue feet to bottom of legs.
Hang with yarn or string.

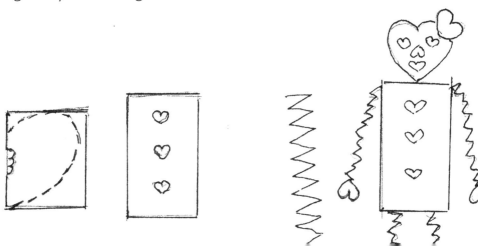

VALENTINE HEART DOG

Articles Needed:

Red construction paper
Pink construction paper
White construction paper
Brown crayon or magic marker
Scissors
Glue

Using red construction paper, cut out red valentine.
Using pink construction paper, cut out two narrow pink hearts.
Invert red heart for head.
Invert pink hearts and glue on either side of head for ears.
Cut out two small white hearts for eyes.
Cut out two very small pink hearts for center of eyes.
Cut out one small pink heart for nose and invert.
Cut out one small wide pink heart for mouth.
Put brown polka dots around nose.

MARCH

1. THE IRISH A WASHERWOMAN

If there Is one tune that announces the stereotype of Irishness, it Is The Irish Washerwoman. Used as background music for performances of every kind. from the stage-Irish caricature of Old Mother Riley in Music Hall days to the famous 'Irish' movie The Quiet Man starring John Wayne. It has long been the best known of all Irish jigs. Yet, in spite of apparent overexposure, it remains perennially popular with fiddlers and was recorded as recently as 1991 by Paddy Glackin on his album In Full Space (Gael-Linn CEFCDI53). The bowing here is one-stroke-to-a-note. The two quavers before the first bar-line (known as pick-up notes) are not accented.

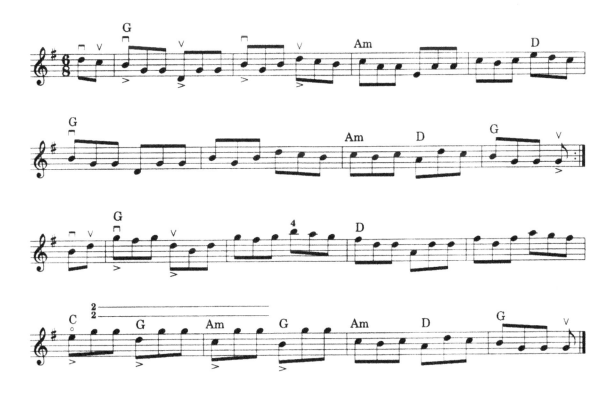

LEPRACHAUN

Articles Needed:

> Blue construction paper
> Brown construction paper
> Green construction paper
> Orange construction paper
> Yellow construction paper
> White construction paper
> Black construction paper
> White cotton for beard
> Crayons
> Scissors
> Glue

Use blue construction paper for background.

Cut out an uneven piece of brown construction paper the width of the blue paper and about 2" high.

Glue this brown paper to the bottom edge of the blue paper for ground.

Using green construction paper, draw and cut out a green Leprachaun.

Cut out orange oval for his face.

Glue orange oval to body.

Glue white cotton around face for a beard.

Using black crayon, draw in belt and buckle on jacket and shoes.

Using green construction paper draw a top hat.

Cut out hat and color in band and buckle around hat.

Draw in eyes, nose and mouth.

Using orange construction paper, draw two hands.

Cut out hands and glue to jacket.

Glue Leprachaun on 1eft side of blue construction paper, standing on ground.

Using white construction paper, color in a rainbow and cut out.

Glue rainbow from the Leprachaun to the other side of the paper.
Using black construction paper, draw and cut out a black pot.
Glue pot at the end of the rainbow, on the right side.
Using yellow paper, cut out small yellow circles for gold coins.
Glue coins inside of top of pot and overflowing onto ground.

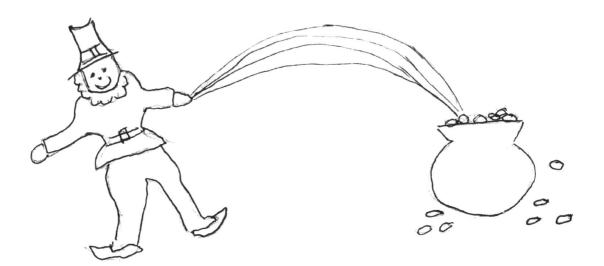

STORY OR POEM

Articles Needed:

A poem or story about March wind
Blue construction paper
White or gray construction paper
Black crayon
Lined paper
Pencil
Scissors
Glue

Read story or poem about March wind.
Using white or gray construction paper, draw a fluffy cloud-like wind.
Cut out face.
Using black crayon, draw in eyes closed and purse lips to look as if they are blowing.
Glue onto blue construction paper.
Using crayon make long streaks coming from mouth to look like breath.
Write two sentences about the March wind.

POEM

Articles Needed:

    March poem coming in like a lion and going out like a lamb
    Run poem off on computer
    Blue construction paper
    White construction paper
    Yellow construction paper
    Small pieces of yellow and brown yarn
    Cotton balls
    Crayons
    Scissors
    Glue

Use blue construction paper for background.
Using yellow construction paper, draw head of lion with ears.
Using brown crayon color in eyes, nose and mouth.
Using the small pieces of yarn, fluff open and mix colors together and glue around face for mane.
Using white construction paper, draw entire lamb, side view.
Color in eyes, nose and mouth areas.
Glue small pieces of cotton onto lamb to look like fur.
Glue lion to upper left corner of blue construction paper.
Glue lamb to lower right corner of construction paper, with nose facing right edge.
If poem is small enough to fit in center of blue construction paper, glue it there.
If not, glue poem to bottom of blue construction paper.

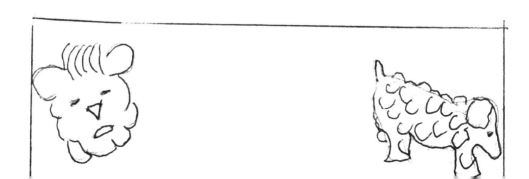

APRIL

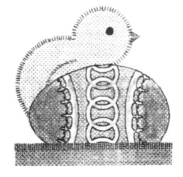

EASTER RABBITS TO USE WITH BASKET CART

Articles Needed:

       Various colored construction paper—Spring colors
       Pencil
       Scissors
       Pencil
       Magic Marker
       Brass fasteners
       Glue

Cut out two upright rabbits, the same color, from construction paper.
Lay rabbits facing each other and trace a jacket of different color, to fit each rabbit.
Glue jacket on each rabbit as they face each other.
Cut out two bows of yet another color and glue on rabbits and jackets at neck area.
Glue a small yellow circle to back tail of each jacket for buttons.
Using Magic Marker draw in eye on each rabbit.
Cut very thin strips of paper for whiskers.
Glue whiskers to each rabbit, between nose and mouth.
Set aside to use with basket.

PATTERN

CART FOR RABBITS

Using 8" x 10" construction paper and holding it horizontally, fold in about 2" from each edge, top and bottom.

Hold paper vertically and fold in about 1 ¾" from each end.

Holding paper vertically, cut on folded line up to horizontal fold, top and bottom, left and right sides.

Holding paper vertically, bend in each side.

Glue each to form box.

Cut two circles of another color for wheels.

Cut two strips of paper, 1" wide by 10" long.

Using brass fastener connect wheel and end of strip to cart on both sides.

Joining rabbits at paws, connect paws with brass fastener to other end of strip which has been placed between paws.

Fill cart with Easter grass and candy

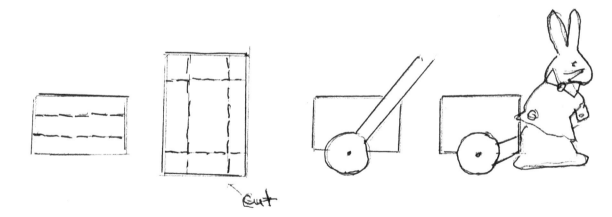

Cut

CHICK

Articles Needed:

     White construction paper
     Yellow construction paper
     Black Magic Marker
     Brass fastener
     Scissors

Using white construction paper, cut out a large oval for egg.
Cut oval in half using jagged cuts to imitate cracked egg.
Join together at bottom, overlapping ends slightly and fasten with a brass fastener.
Using yellow construction paper, draw and cut out top half of a yellow chick.
Using black Magic Marker put an eye on chick.
Open egg and fasten chick to egg at bottom, using the same brass fastener.
Egg can open and close, hiding or showing chick.

EASTER EGG BALLOON

Articles Needed:

      Round balloon
      Various Spring colored tissue paper
      Liquid starch
      Newspaper
      Toothpick
      String
      Pin
      Glitter
      Glue

Blow up round balloon.
Cut various colored strips of tissue paper about 1" in width and 6" in length.
Spread newspaper and fill bowl with liquid starch.
Dip each strip of tissue in bowl of liquid starch and lay on and around balloon.
Cover balloon completely, overlapping and going in different directions.
When completely covered, make certain strips on balloon are completely wet and lying flat against balloon.
Let dry overnight.
When completely dry, puncture balloon with a pin and remove balloon from inside of paper egg.
Tie a toothpick to one end of a 2" length of string.
Place toothpick lengthwise in top hole of egg.
Decorate with glue and glitter if desire.

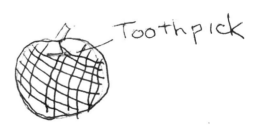

Toothpick

EASTER EGG TREE

Articles Needed:

Small branch or branches from a tree
Coffee can
Soil
Crepe paper or construction paper
Uncooked eggs
Egg dye or food coloring
Various desired decorations—candies, sprinkles, glitter, ribbon, construction
   paper cutouts.
Needle
Toothpick
Thread

Place small branch or branches in coffee can filled with soil.
Cover can with construction paper or crepe paper and glue to hold.
Puncture a small hole at each end of a raw egg.
Blow out inside of egg.
Handle gently and color and decorate egg.
Tie a 6" piece of thread to a half toothpick.
Insert toothpick in hole at one end of egg.
Tie thread with egg to branch of tree.
Cover tree with various colored and decorated eggs, using various lengths of thread.

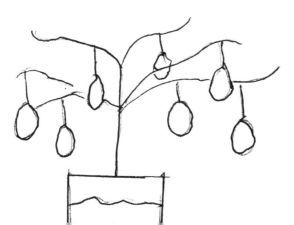

MAY

LILAC FLOWERS

Articles Needed:

Purple paint
White paint
Green paint
Brown paint
Color of choice of paint for vase
Gray bogus paper or manilla paper
Brushes

Using choice of color, shape decorate and paint vase at center of bottom of paper.

Using purple paint which has been mixed with white paint to make various shades of purple, start at top of paper and dab paint gently to form tiny petals of lilac flower.

Shape flower, smaller at top to larger at bottom.

Overlap some of the tiny petals in various shades of the purple and white paint.

Using brown paint, paint a thin stem from lilac flower down into vase.

Using green, paint, paint a few small broad leaves on stem.

Form a bouquet, painting several lilacs for the vase.

LILACS

Articles Needed:

> White construction paper
> Various shades of purple crepe paper
> White crepe paper
> Green crepe paper
> Color of choice of construction paper for vase
> Brown paint
> scissors
> Glue

Using choice of color of construction paper, draw and cut out vase and glue to center and bottom of paper. Do not glue top of vase so that stems can be placed inside of vase.

Using various shades of purple crepe paper and white crepe paper, cut out tiny circles.

Roll circles into small balls.

Glue various colored small balls on construction paper, forming shape of lilac flower, starting small at top and becoming broader at bottom.

Fill in all spaces and overlap to give three dimensional and upraised look.

Paint long brown sterns from lilac flower, going into vase.

Place a few green leaves, made from crepe paper, on sterns.

Make a bouquet for the vase.

DAFFODIL

Articles Needed:

    Blue construction paper
    Yellow construction paper
    Green construction paper
    Pencil
    Scissors
    Glue

Using yellow construction paper, draw five petals like a star.
Cut out the five petals.
Cut a large hole in the center of the star.
Roll a ¾" x 1 ¼" piece of yellow paper and glue together to form a tube.
Cut small slits around one end of tube and insert in hole.
Bend down slits and glue to under part of star.
Cut other edge around to make fringe of flower.
Bend down slightly.
Make green stem and two long pointed green leaves.
Glue leaves on stem.
Glue stem to under part of flower.
Glue flower to blue construction paper.

TULIPS

Articles Needed:

      Blue construction paper
      Red or yellow construction paper
      Green construction paper
      Scissors
      Glue

Using red or yellow construction paper, cut out three petals for each tulip.
Cut two of the petals the same size.
Cut the center petal larger than the other.
Glue the two petals to the blue construction paper, one on the left and one on the right, leaving space in the center for the larger petal.
Fold the larger petal in half vertically and glue edges and place in center, between the left and right petal, to look three dimensional.
Using green construction paper make green stem and two long, thin leaves.
Glue stem and leaves to flower and then on to blue construction paper.

MAYPOLE

Articles Needed:

    Volley ball standard or flag pole
    17 various colored crepe paper streamers, 2" wide, and full length of paper
    17 children or adults
    Tape recorder
    Appropriate musical tape

Tape securely, 17 various colored pieces of crepe paper, to top of standard or pole.

Place 10 children on outside of circle with 10 crepe paper streamers, facing clock-wise.

Place 7 children on inside of circle with 7 crepe paper streamers, facing counter clock-wise.

Put tape in tape recorder and when music starts begin to go around pole intertwining strips of crepe paper.

When it is all wound, each group reverses direction to unwind and come back to original position.

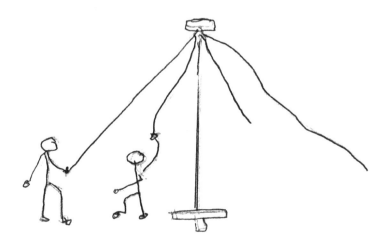

MOTHER'S DAY SILHOUETTE

Articles Needed:

> White construction paper
> Black construction paper
> Film Projector
> Chair
> Wall or blackboard
> Pencil
> Scissors
> Glue

Tape large, white construction paper to wall or blackboard.

Using film projector, shine light on white paper on wall or blackboard.

Sit person sidewards on chair between blackboard or wall and film projector, casting the shape of head on the paper.

Sit very still.

Trace around view of head on white paper.

Cut head out and glue to a piece of black construction paper.

May reverse colors—black on white.

FLAG

Articles Needed:

> White construction paper
> Red paint
> Blue paint
> White paint
> Brushes
> Paper stars (optional)

Hold white construction paper horizontally.

Paint seven red stripes on white construction paper.

Start one at top along edge and one along bottom edge.

Leave same amount of white paper showing and paint two more red stripes, one from top and one from bottom.

Paint two more in same manner, leaving last stripe to go evenly in between others.

Let dry.

Paint a rectangle of blue in upper left corner, a little less than half the width of flag and long enough to cover middle red stripe.

Let dry.

Paint fifty white dots for stars or glue fifty large paper stars in field of blue background.

MAY BASKETS

Articles Needed:

      Spring colored construction paper
      Brass fastener or stapler
      Scissors
      Crayons

Cut construction paper into square.
Keep small piece left over for handle.
Fold square in half diagonally, making a triangle.
Fold square in half opposite way, making a triangle.
Open paper and fold piece of paper in half, bottom to top.
While paper is in half, cut small fringe across top of paper, opposite fold, from left to right.
Holding paper, push in both right and left sides.
Holding points of sides together, staple or use a brass fastener to join the points and the ends of the small piece of paper for a handle, together.
Flatten basket and decorate both sides with crayons.
Fill with small flowers, if desired.

JUNE

FATHER'S DAY SHIRT AND TIE

Articles Needed:

   White construction paper
   Shirt buttons
   Construction paper
   Scissors
   Glue

Using white construction paper and holding it vertically, bend top back about 1 ½"

Holding vertically bend each side to meet each other in center, forming shirt and crease down on fold.

Pull left corner of folded piece down and to the left to make the points of a collar.

Do the same to the right side.

Cut a strip of white construction paper 2" wide and the length of the front of the shirt.

Glue strip to front of shirt over edges that meet in center.

Glue shirt buttons down the front.

Using construction paper, cut two pieces of paper 12" x 3" wide.

Shape pieces so that bottom of each is wider than top.

Shape wider parts at bottom into points like a tie.

Glue pieces, one on top of the other, at top of shirt only, between collar, and let hang loose.

Cut a small circle from construction paper for a knot.

Glue to top of tie.

Can use as card for a gift for father.

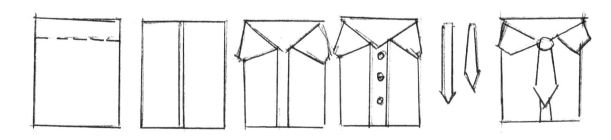

CIRCUS DOG

Articles Needed:

       Art paper on roll—white or black preferably
       White or black paint
       Red paint
       Brushes
       Scissors
       Pencil
       Glue

Using art paper, draw a poodle dog sitting upright.
Cut out.
Paint dog white or black, if not using white or black paper.
Paint in white or black eye.
Paint red collar on dog.
Draw and cut out stool for dog to sit on.
Decorate stool.
Glue dog to stool.

CIRCUS SEAL

Articles Needed:

> Art paper on roll-black preferably
> Black paint
> White paint
> Choice of color construction paper
> Scissors
> Brushes
> Glue

Using art paper, draw a seal with nose up in *air*.
Draw flippers.
Cut out.
Paint seal black, if not using black paper.
Paint in white eye.
Cut very thin strips of gray construction paper for whiskers.
Glue to seal nose.
Draw and cut out stool for seal to set on.
Decorate stool.
Glue seal to stool.
Draw a round circle for a ball, using choice of color of construction paper cut out and glue to seal's nose.

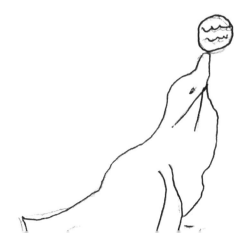

CIRCUS DOG

Articles Needed:

      Art paper on roll—white or black preferably
      White or black paint
      Pink crepe paper or any choice of color
      Hula hoop
      Pencil
      Scissors
      Brushes
      Glue

Using art paper, draw a poodle dog in running position, front legs forward and back legs going back.

Paint dog white or black, if not using white or black paper.

Cut a strip of crepe paper to fit dog for a skirt.

Place crepe paper on bottom part of body.

Make a crepe paper bow and glue to dog's head.

Wind 1" wide crepe paper around hula hoop.

Place dog half way through hula hoop.

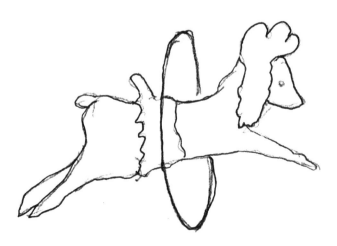

TRAPEZE ARTIST

Articles Needed:

    Art paper on roll
    Various colored paint
    Crepe paper
    Yarn
    Scissors
    Pencil
    Glue
    15" dowel stick or piece of bamboo
    Two pieces of clothes line

Using large piece of art paper, lay on floor with arms upraised.
Have someone trace around form or draw form freehand.
Cut out form.
Paint in skin colors and put in eyes, nose and mouth.
Paint on clothes or use crepe paper for a tutu for a ballerina.
Place yarn on head for hair and glue in place.
Paint on shoes or use crepe paper for slippers or leave bare.
Tie ropes to either end of stick for a trapeze.
Hang person with hands wrapped around stick and taped in place.
Hang or tape to wall.

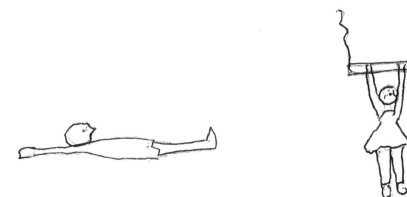

TIGHT ROPE WALKER

Articles Needed:

      Art paper on roll
      Various colored paints
      Crepe paper
      Yarn
      Pencil
      Scissors
      Glue
      Clothes line

Using large Art paper, lay on side with one arm forward and one arm back, one leg forward and one leg back.

Have someone trace around form or draw form freehand.

Cut out form.

Paint in skin colors and decorate with eye, nose and mouth.

Place yarn on head for hair and glue in place.

Paint on clothes or use crepe paper for a tutu for a ballerina.

Paint or use crepe paper for ballerina shoes.

Can trace arm in an upright position, if desire her to carry an umbrella.

Make umbrella shape and a handle and cut out.

Decorate umbrella in various colors using paint or crepe paper.

Attach umbrella to upright hand of ballerina

Place ballerina or man on clothes walker.

Tape on wall or hang.

ICE CREAM CLOWN

Articles Needed:

       Wafer cup or cone shaped ice cream cones
       Ice cream
       Gum drops
       Red hots
       Paper plate

Using wafer cup or cone-shaped cone, place scoop of ice cream on cone.
Place in freezer.
When hard, decorate as a clown face with hots and gum drops.
Dip hots and gum drops in icing to make stick, if desire.
Place on paper party plate.
Place in freezer to harden.

CLOWN

Articles Needed:

Large sheet of art paper on roll
Various colored construction paper
Various colored paints
White paint
Various colored tissue or crepe paper
Paint
Any other creative, decorative materials
Pencil or dark crayon
Various colored Yarn
String
Glue

Using large sheet of art paper, draw large clown making full arms and legs to look like clown suit.

Can draw clown with one arm up to hold balloons.

Child or adult can lay on paper and with pencil or crayon, can trace around form leaving ample space around to look like clown suit.

Cut out form.

Decorate suit with paints, tissue, crepe paper, or any other decorative designs.

Paint white face on clown.

Decorate face, putting in eyes, nose, mouth.

Put yarn on for hair, placing it down the sides to cover ears.

Draw a desired hat from construction paper to fit head.

Cut out and decorate as desired.

Using any color desired, draw a pair of very large shoes.

Cut out and place each shoe going in opposite direction.

Glue to bottom of clown's legs.

Using desired colored construction paper, trace around each hand and cut out.

JULY

FOURTH OF JULY

Articles Needed:

      Cake mix
      Vanilla icing
      Cupcake tins
      Cupcake liners
      Red, white, blue confetti sugars
      Small American flags.

Follow recipe on box of cake mix.
Place in cupcake tins lined with liners.
When baked, remove and let cool.
Decorate with vanilla icing and sprinkle with colored confetti sugars.
Place small American flags in center.

PLAY CLAY

Articles Needed:

       Arm and Hammer Baking soda (1 lb. pkg.)
       1 cup cornstarch
       1 ¼ cups cold water

Stir together baking soda and cornstarch in saucepan.
Add water and cook over medium heat, stirring constantly.
When mixture is consistency of moist mashed potatoes
(approx. 10-15 minutes, turn out on a plate.
Cover with a damp cloth.
When Play Clay is cool enough to handle, pat until smooth, and use.
Unused portions can be sealed in a tightly sealed plastic bag in refrigerator.
Bring to room temperature before using.
Rollout clay to ¼ inch thickness on waxed paper.
Cut with cookie cutters into circles, stars, Christmas or animal shapes.
Use a toothpick to press a hole near top for hanging ornament with a string.

FOURTH OF JULY JELLO

Articles Needed:

Large box of strawberry, cherry or raspberry Jello.
8 x 10 dish
Knife
Jello cups
Whipping cream
Small American flags

Dissolve Jello according to directions for very firm jello.
Place in dish that would make Jello 1" in depth.;
Place in refrigerator until very firm.
Slice into cubes and place some cubes in individual cups.
Top each cup with whipping cream.
Place small American flag in center of each cup.

CIRCLES AND SPIRALS

Articles Needed:

    Construction paper
    Scissors
    String
    Paper clip
    Straight pin

Using construction paper, make a circle as large as the paper.

Cut out circle and continue to cut into circle, getting smaller and smaller with no interruption, until center is reached.

Tie straight pin at one end of string and paper clip at other end.

Open paper clip and hang spiral.

SEPTEMBER

LEAVES FOR WINDOWS

Articles Needed:

      Various Types of leaves
      Book or magazine
      Construction paper
      Newspaper
      Stapler
      Waxed paper
      Iron
      Scissors
      Tape

Collect Various types of leaves from trees out of doors.
Press leaves for a few days between pages of a book or magazine.
Layout newspaper.
Cut two pieces of waxed paper about 15" in width and lay on newspaper.
Lay assorted leaves between two pieces of waxed paper.
Press with a hot iron until waxed paper sticks together.
Trim around edges of waxed paper to make even.
Cut two strips of construction paper 2" x 15".
Cut two strips of construction paper 2" in width and the height of the waxed paper.
Form a frame around waxed paper and staple in corners.
Tape onto window where light shines through.

LEAVES

Articles Needed:

      Collection of different leaves
      Plain newsprint
      Various colored crayons

Lay leaves on newspaper with spaces between leaves.
Cover with plain newsprint.
Rub each leaf gently with a different color of crayon.
When finished use as birthday wrap.

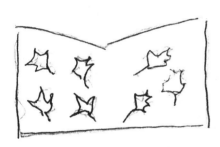 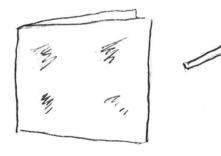

LEAVES FOR DECORATION

Articles Needed:

      Various types of leaves
      Book *or* magazine
      Various Fall colored construction paper
      Pencil
      Scissors
      Thumbtacks, tape or glue

Collect various types of leaves from trees out of doors.
Press leaves for a few days between pages of a book or magazine.
Trace various leaves with pencil onto Fall colored construction paper.
Cut out.
Tape, thumbtack or glue leaves as desired for decorations.

RECIPE FOR DOUGH ART

      1 cup of salt
      2 cups of flour
      1 cup of water

Mix together thoroughly and shape as you desire.
Bake at 325 degrees until light brown.
Paint any color.

LEAF COLLECTION BOOKLET

Articles Needed:

        Collection of various leaves and their seeds, if possible
        Books or magazines
        Construction paper or plain manilla paper
        Magic Marker
        Glue
        Stapler

Collect various leaves and their seeds.
Press leaves between heavy books or magazines
Glue each pressed leaf and its seed on a piece of construction paper or manilla paper.
Identify each leaf and label at bottom of page.
Make a booklet of the leaves and staple together.
Use a piece of construction paper for a cover.
Give booklet a title.

SCHOOL BUS

Articles Needed:

> Yellow construction paper
> Black construction paper
> Magic Marker or Crayons
> Scissors
> Pencil
> Glue

Using yellow construction paper draw a school bus.
Using black Magic Marker or crayons, draw in windows and a door.
Cut the bus out.
Using black construction paper, draw two circles for wheels.
Place wheels on bus.
Color a head with face in each window of bus.

COLUMBUS' SHIP

Articles Needed:

       wooden skewer
       American cheese
       Grapefruit halve
       Blue construction paper
       Lettuce leaf
       Plate

Insert a piece of cheese through a wooden skewer for a sail and mast.
Insert skewer into half of grapefruit vertically, to represent ship.
Line plate with blue construction paper for water.
Place lettuce leaf on top of blue paper for waves of ocean.
Place grapefruit on top of lettuce leaf.
Use as center piece or at each place setting.
Edible.

OWL

Articles Needed:

Small brown lunch bag
Small piece of brown construction paper
Small piece of yellow construction paper
Small piece of black construction paper
Brown crayon
Newspaper or kleenex tissues
Scissors
Glue
Straight pin
String

Using a small brown lunch bag, keep it closed and flat and invert it, bottom up at top and open end of bag at bottom.

Cut out two small, brown triangles and glue to left and right side of bag at top, for ears.

Cut out two small yellow circles for large eyes and glue to bag, beneath ears.

Cut out two smaller black circles and glue to center of yellow circles for centers of eyes.

Cut out a small yellow triangle for beak of owl.

Hold triangle vertically and crease in half.

Glue to center of bag, beneath eyes and hanging over bottom of bag, for a three dimensional look.

Using a brown crayon, make feathers all over bag.

Use the letter U that looks like feathers when they are grouped together.

Make a 3" cut up the center of the open end of bag.

These are the legs.

Stuff bag with newspaper or whatever desired, but do not fill face of owl.

Tie each leg with a small piece of string.

Tie a piece of string to a straight pin and insert pin in center of head of owl and hang.

WITCH

Articles Needed:

    Paper pie plate
    Black construction paper
    Green construction paper
    Small, long pinecone
    Black crayon
    Pencil
    Scissors
    Glue
    String to hang witch

Using the underside of a pie plate, place the pie plate on black construction paper and draw a pointed hat the width of the pie plate.

Cut out pointed hat and glue to top of pie plate.

Insert pointed pinecone in center of pie plate for a nose and glue around edges so it holds.

Using green construction paper, cut out a down-turned mouth.

Glue mouth to pie plate.

Using green or black construction paper, cut two 2" wide by 10" strips of paper.

Cut each strip into large slices to represent hair.

Glue to top of pie plate and on either side of face.

Using green construction paper, cut two small ovals for eyes.

Glue eyes onto pie plate.

Place small black circle in center of each eye, using crayon.

Make a hole in the top of the pie plate and tie string.

Hang witch by string.

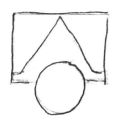

BLACK CAT

Articles Needed:

    Black construction paper
    Small piece of green construction paper
    Black crayon
    Scissors
    Pencil
    Glue

Using black construction paper, cut out oval.
Cut out two small black triangles for ears.
Glue ears on top of oval on the left and right sides.
Holding black construction paper vertically, cut a 1" long strip of paper.
Fold strip back and forth in a fan fold.
Glue strip for a neck at center and bottom of oval.
Using green construction paper cut out two ovals for eyes.
Glue eyes to oval.
Using black crayon color in a small black circle in each eye.
Using green construction paper, cut out two small green triangles for nose and mouth.
Invert nose and glue on oval.
Glue triangle for mouth.
Cut out very thin strips of green paper for whiskers.
Glue whiskers on oval below nose.
Using full sheet of black construction paper fold in half just at top to find center of paper.
    Cut out haunches for cat, shaping like a heart and each paw going out to left and right sides.
    Glue haunches to bottom of neck of cat.
    Tape or hang cat when finished.

GHOST

Articles Needed:

White tissue paper or white kleenex
Extra tissue or kleenex
String or yarn
Small piece of black construction paper
Scissors
Glue
Straight pin
String about 2 feet long

Roll a piece of kleenex or tissue paper into a ball.
Using a large piece of tissue paper or kleenex, place ball in center of tissue or kleenex.
Gather under ball and tie with string around neck area
Fluff out bottom to look like ghost.
Cut out two small, black circles for eyes.
Glue to head.
Tie 2 foot string to the center of a straight pin.
Pin straight pin to center of head of ghost and hang.

MAN'S PILGRIM HAT

Articles Needed:

        Black construction paper
        Yellow crayon
        Scissors
        Pencil
        Glue or stapler

Using black construction paper, fold in half just at top and center and pinch to find center.
Cut shape of hat and make brim of hat at bottom of paper on both sides.
Draw band and buckle above brim of hat.
Color buckle yellow.
Cut out a 1" strip of black paper to fit around head.
Glue or staple strip to each side of the hat and to the back of the hat, behind brim.

 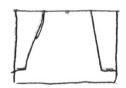 

Back View

LADY'S PILGRIM HAT

Articles Needed:

   White construction paper
   Stapler

Using white construction paper and holding it horizontally / fold the lower bottom of paper up, about 1 ½".

Still holding it horizontally, bend paper in half so that top portion of paper comes to a point and sides meet at the points and in the back.

Staple where the points meet.

 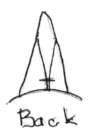 

Back   Front

INDIAN MAN'S HEAD

Articles Needed:

Orange construction paper
Black construction paper
Brown construction paper
Various colored construction paper
Scissors
Pencil
Crayons or Magic Marker
Glue

Using orange construction paper, cut an oval the size of the paper, for a head.

Using black construction paper, lay orange oval on black paper and trace around top half of oval for hair, so hair fits head.

Cut out hair.

Using brown construction paper, cut a strip about 4" wide and long enough to fit around man's head, for a band.

Fold paper strip in half lengthwise and decorate with indian designs, using various colored markers or crayons.

Using various colored construction paper, cut strips about 3" wide by 12" in length.

Fold paper strips in half and holding fold, round off top end towards fold, to make a Point.

Hold the fold and make short cuts with scissors along the edge, from top to bottom, to look like a feather.

Glue each feather side by side inside fold of brown band.

Place band around head as a headpiece and glue to back of head.

Decorate face with eyes, nose and mouth, using crayons or Magic Markers.

Make it look like warpaint.

INDIAN LADY'S HEAD

Articles Needed:

Orange construction paper
Black construction paper
Brown construction paper
Yellow construction paper
Scissors
Pencil
Crayons or Magic Marker
Glue

Using orange construction paper, cut an oval the size of the paper for a head.

Using black construction paper, lay orange oval on black paper and trace around top half of oval for hair. so hair fits head.

Cut out and shape an indent in center of black paper.

Glue black hair on top of oval.

Cut out two strips of black paper, 2" wide and length of paper.

Holding strips together, scallop one entire side and then the other, starting about two inches from end.

These will be braids and the two inches will be the ends of hair.

Shape ends of hair.

Glue braids in the back on each side of the head.

Cut out or color in eyes, nose and mouth.

Using brown construction paper, cut a strip about 4" wide, and long enough to fit around lady's head, for a band.

Fold paper strip in half lengthwise and decorate with indian designs, using various colored markers or crayons.

Using yellow construction paper cut a 3" wide strip of paper by 12" in length.

Fold strip in half and holding fold, round off top end towards fold, to make a point.

Hold the fold and make short cuts with scissors along the edge, from top to bottom, to look like a feather.

Glue feather inside fold of band and in center of band.

Place around head as a headpiece and glue to back of head.

PILGRIM LADY

Articles Needed:

Orange construction paper
Yellow, brown or black construction paper
White construction paper
Crayons or Magic Markers
Scissors
Stapler
Pencil
Glue

Using orange construction paper, cut an oval the size of the paper, for a head.
Using yellow, brown or black construction paper, lay oval on top of paper for hair.
Trace around top half of head so hair fits head.
Cut out and shape and indent or cut bangs in the front.
Glue to oval for hair.
Using white construction paper and holding it horizontally, fold up lower bottom of paper about 1 ½"
Bend paper in half so that top portion of paper comes to a point and staple where sides meet together at points.
Fit on oval head and glue in back to head.
Cut out or draw in eyes, nose and mouth with crayon or Magic Markers.

 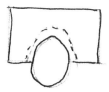

PILGRIM MAN

Articles Needed:

    Orange construction paper
    Brown or black construction paper
    Black construction paper
    Crayons or Magic Markers
    Scissors
    Stapler
    Pencil
    Glue

Using orange construction paper, cut an oval the size of the paper, for a head.

Using brown or black construction paper, lay oval on top of paper for hair.

Trace around top half of head so hair fits head and let sides of black or brown paper remain to be long hair for man. May leave bangs for man.

Cut out and glue to oval for hair.

Using black construction paper, fold in half just at the top of paper and pinch to find center.

Cut shape as a Pilgrim hat and make brim on left and right side of hat.

Glue hat to oval head.

Using Magic Markers or crayon, decorate with band and buckle.

 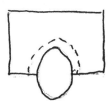 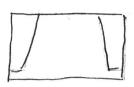 

TURKEY

Articles Needed:

> Red construction paper
> Brown construction paper
> Yellow construction paper
> Package of brown crepe paper
> Scissors
> Pencil
> Glue

Using brown construction paper, cut out an oval large as the paper.

Cut strips of brown crepe paper about 1 ½" wide and length of package of crepe paper.

Flute both sides of the strips of crepe paper.

Starting along the outer edge of the oval, glue crepe paper, round oval and overlapping so that brown construction paper does not show through.

Work to center and cover center.

Using red construction paper, cut out a small oval for head of turkey.

Using black Magic Marker or black crayon, color in an eye on each side of head.

Cut out small waddle and glue under bottom of head.

Cut out two red strips of paper ½" wide and 5" long.

Hold strips together like an L and alternately fold over each until a spring is made.

Glue one end of spring to back of head and other end to center of body of turkey.

Using yellow construction paper, cut out two strips of paper ¼" wide and 4" in length.

Glue strips to bottom of turkey's body for legs.

Using yellow construction paper cut out two small triangles and glue to bottom of turkeys legs for feet.

Cut out to form three toes on each foot.

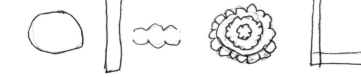

HAND TURKEY

Articles Needed:

> Plain paper
> Hand
> Pencil
> Crayons
> Scissors

Lay hand on paper.
Spread hand with thumb far from other four fingers.
Trace around hand and fingers.
Color in four fingers with different colored crayons as feathers.
Color the thumb in red for head of turkey.
Cut out if desire.

INDIAN PRINCESS HAT

Articles Needed:

Brown wrapping paper or brown paper bag
Colored construction paper
Crayons or Magic Marker
Scissors
Stapler
Pencil
Glue

Using brown wrapping paper or paper bag cut a strip of paper about 6" in width and long enough to fit around head.

Fold paper in half, lengthwise.

Decorate with Indian designs, using crayons or Magic Markers.

Using a piece of construction paper, cut a 3" wide strip of paper the entire length of paper.

Fold strip in half and holding fold, round off top end towards fold, to make a point.

Hold the fold and make short cuts with scissors, along the edge, from top to bottom, to look like a feather.

Glue feather inside of fold and in center of brown paper.

Fit to head and staple ends together overlapping slightly in back.

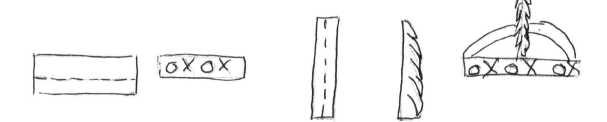

INDIAN CHIEF HEADPIECE

Articles Needed:

      Brown wrapping paper or brown paper bag
      Various colored construction paper
      Crayons or Magic Marker
      Scissors
      Stapler
      Pencil
      Glue

Using brown wrapping paper or paper bag, cut a strip of paper about 6" in width and long enough to fit around head and hang down in back for a tail.

Fold paper in half, lengthwise.

Decorate with Indian designs, using crayons or Magic Markers.

Using various colored construction paper, cut 3" wide strips of paper the entire length of paper.

Fold strips in half and holding fold, round off top end towards fold, to make a point.

Hold the fold and make short cuts with scissors along the edge, from top to bottom, to look like a feather.

Glue each feather side by side inside fold of brown paper, the entire length of paper.

Fit to head and staple together, allowing tail to hang down.

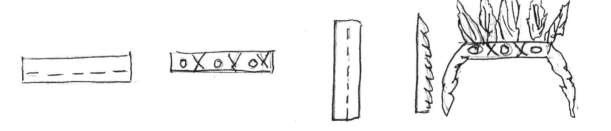

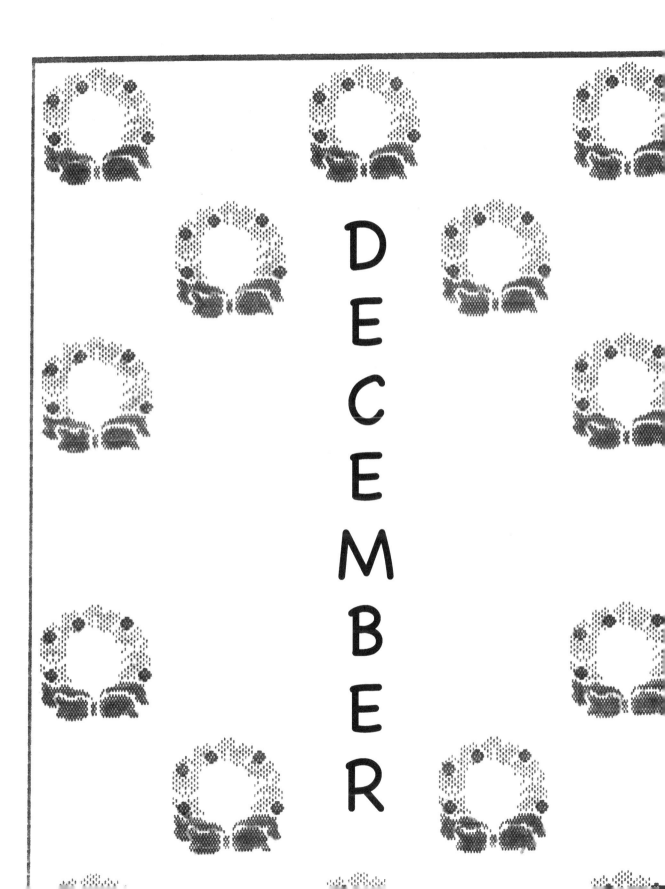

CHAINS

Articles Needed:

> Red construction paper
> Green construction paper
> Scissors
> Glue

Using red and green construction paper, hold vertically and cut 1" strips of paper.
Glue ends of one strip together.
Slip different colored strips through each ring and glue ends together, forming a long chain.
Decorate tree or room with chain.

RUDOLPH

Articles Needed:

    Brown construction paper
    White construction paper
    Black construction paper
    Red construction paper
    Stapler
    Scissors
    Glue

Using brown construction paper and holding it horizontally, bend in half to form a point in center and bend in left and right sides, overlapping ends.

Staple ends together. This is the head.

Using brown construction paper, draw two long antlers.

Cut antlers out and glue to front of head of reindeer, one on each side.

Using white construction paper, cut out two circles for eyes of reindeer.

Glue eyes to face of reindeer.

Using black construction paper, cut out two smaller black circles for centers of eyes.

Glue black centers of eyes to center of white circles.

Using black construction paper, cut two strips about 2" long and ½" wide for eyelashes.

Make small cuts on the strips and glue over the eyes.

Using red construction paper, make a round circle and cut out.

Glue to point of face for a nose.

Use Rudolph as a card holder.

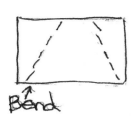

Bend

ANGEL

Articles Needed:

      White construction paper
      Orange, beige or brown construction paper
      Small piece of yellow construction paper
      Magic Markers or crayons
      Pencil
      Scissors
      Glue

Using white construction paper, hold horizontally.
Bend bottom of paper up to center of paper and crease on fold.
Cut off on fold.
Using larger white piece, bend in on each side, forming point at top.
Staple together in back where sides come together and overlap slightly. This is the robe.
Using orange, beige or brown construction paper, cut small oval for head.
Using Magic Marker or crayon, color in hair, eyes, nose and mouth.
Glue head to front of point of robe.
Using small piece cut off from white construction paper and holding it vertically, cut a 1" strip the entire length of paper.
Place strip around back of robe and joining in front, for arms.
Glue together where they meet in front.
Using orange, beige or brown construction paper, cut two hands, as if praying and glue together.
Cut two feet and glue to bottom of robe.
Using small piece of yellow construction paper, form a circle and cut out center for a halo.
Cut small yellow stem and glue onto halo.
Glue halo to back of angel's head and bend halo down over head.
Cut off points of robe to permit angel to stand.

CHEERIO CHAIN

Articles Needed:

    Cheerio cereal
    Needle
    Thread

Using Cheerio cereal, string cereal on thread with needle.
Hang strings of Cheerio on Christmas tree for decoration

POPCORN

Articles Needed:

    Popcorn
    Popcorn popper
    Needle
    Thread

Pop popcorn in popper or buy already popped.
Using needle and long thread, thread popcorn on long thread.
Use for decoration on Christmas tree.

CRANBERRIES

Articles Needed:

  Cranberries
  Needle
  Thread

Using needle and thread, thread cranberries on long thread.
Use for decoration on Christmas tree.

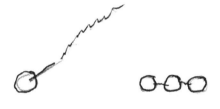

SANTA ENVELOPE

Articles Needed:

      Orange or beige construction paper
      Red construction paper
      Black construction paper
      White construction paper
      Yellow construction paper
      Blue construction paper
      Magic Markers or crayons
      Pencil
      Scissors
      Glue

Using two pieces of large red construction paper, cut out two large red circles.
Cut one circle in half.
Glue a half circle around edges but NOT on edge that was cut.
Place half circle on whole circle to form pocket or pouch.
Using beige or orange paper, draw a smaller circle for Santa's head.
Cut out and glue to center of single red circle.
Using black construction paper, cut a strip out about 2" wide and long enough to cover cut half of circle from left to right sides. This is a belt.
Using yellow construction paper, cut out a buckle to go over center of black belt.
Using red construction paper cut out a stocking hat to fit Santa's head.
Bend end over and glue to center of hat.
Trim edge of hat around face with white construction paper for a fur band.
Using white construction paper fit paper around face for a mustache and beard.
Glue to face.
Cut beard into strips and curl each strip with a pencil.
Using black construction paper, cut two mittens, with thumbs up, and glue on Santa's stomach.

Using blue construction paper, cut two circles for eyes.
Glue eyes on face.
Using red construction paper, cut round circle for nose.
Glue nose to face, above mustache.
Using white construction paper cut out two eyebrows and glue over eyes.
Use Santa as a card holder.

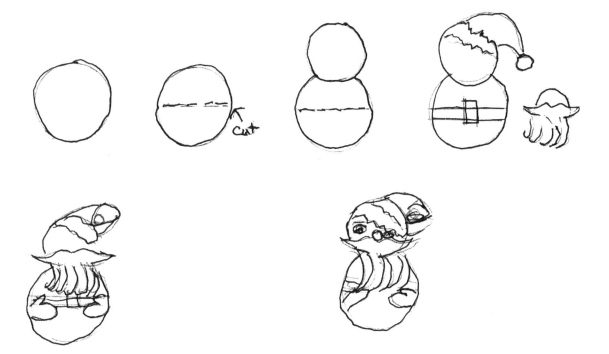

CHRISTMAS TREE

Articles Needed:

        Green construction paper
        Various colored construction paper
        Magic Marker
        Glitter, if desired
        Scissors
        Glue

Using green construction paper, hold paper vertically and fold in half.

Hold fold and cut from bottom to top, beginning at fold side.

Cut outwards to outer edge for each branch, making each branch larger, until you reach top of paper with the largest branch.

Cut in and form trunk.

Cut round circles for Christmas balls, using various colored construction paper.

Decorate with Magic Marker or glitter.

Glue on tree.

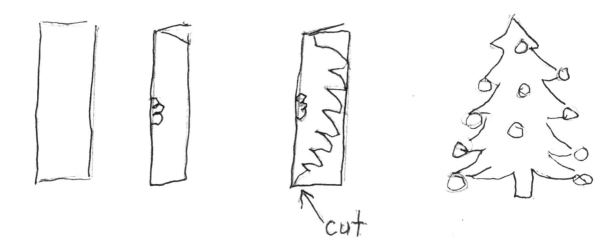

cut

HANUKKAH—THE MENORAH

Judah Maccabee and the other Jews who took part in the rededication of the Second Temple witnessed what they believed to be a miracle. Even though there was only enough untainted olive oil to keep the Menorah's candles burning for a single day, the flames continued flickering for eight nights, leaving them time to find a fresh supply. This wondrous event inspired the Jewish sages to proclaim a yearly eight-day festival, which we call Hanukka, "The Festival of Lights".

Materials Needed:

> Four yellow sheets of construction paper
> One orange sheet of construction paper
> One brown sheet of construction paper
> Scissors
> Glue
> One piece of cardboard

Holding yellow construction paper horizontally fold in half and cut in two pieces. Roll each piece into a tube and glue closed. Do this with each of the other yellow pieces.

Do the same to the brown construction paper only making just one candle.

Fold orange construction paper in half and cut with scissors. Fold each of the halves again and cut with scissors. Fold each of these pieces in half. Draw a flame shaped object for light for candles. Glue each flame to a candle.

Fold cardboard in half, length-wise and insert candles inside fold and glue, making four on each side of cardboard and placing brown candle in center making it stand higher than the others. This is the candle that lights all of the rest.

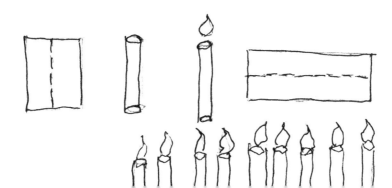

LATKES

Ingredients

> 2 cups peeled and shredded potatoes
> 1 tablespoon grated onion
> 3 eggs, beaten
> 2 tablespoons all purpose flour
> 1 ½ teaspoons salt
> ½ cup peanut oil for frying
> Serve with apple sauce, sour cream and chopped green onions! Happy Hanukkah!

Peel two large potatoes, wash and grate on a grater into a large howl.

Grate one onion on grater and add to the grated potato. Squeeze mixture with hand to remove as much water as possible that has accumulated.

Add eggs beaten and flour and salt. Mix together thoroughly.

Using a frying pan, place oil and heat. Drop Latkes mixture by tablespoon in fry pan and fry until golden brown.

Drain on paper towel. Serve on a plate with applesauce and topped with sour cream and green onions.